Gemini

Horoscope 2024

By
Lyra Asterorion

Table of Contents
Gemini (May 21 - June 20)

Personality

Geminis are one of the most fascinating and complex signs of the zodiac. They are known for their adaptability, curiosity, expressiveness, versatility, social skills, charm, energy, quick wit, restlessness, intellect, changeability, playfulness, inquisitiveness, risk-taking spirit, independent thinking, and social butterfly nature.

Geminis are like chameleons because they can easily blend in with any crowd. They are adaptable and can switch between different roles and situations with ease. They thrive in diverse environments and are quick to adjust to changing circumstances.

Geminis are also incredibly curious. They have a thirst for knowledge and are always eager to learn and explore new topics. They are also excellent communicators. They are articulate, and witty, and often possess a way with words that captivate those around them.

Geminis have a wide range of interests and talents. They are often multi-talented individuals who excel in various areas. They are also social creatures and enjoy interacting with others. They are skilled at networking and forming connections with people from all walks of life.

Geminis are also known for their natural charm and wit. They are engaging conversationalists and know how to put people at ease. They can make friends easily and are often the life of the party.

Geminis have boundless energy and enthusiasm. They are always on the go, seeking new experiences and adventures. They are also quick thinkers and excellent problem solvers.

However, Geminis can also be restless. Their dual nature can lead to a tendency to get bored easily. They may seek novelty and variety in their pursuits. Geminis can also be changeable in their moods and opinions. They may flip-flop on certain issues as they explore different perspectives.

Despite their flaws, Geminis are some of the most entertaining and stimulating people you'll ever meet. They bring a unique perspective to the world and are always up for a challenge. Life with a Gemini is never dull.

Here are some of the key personality traits of Gemini individuals:

Adaptability: Geminis can easily adjust to new situations and people. They are comfortable in a variety of settings and can quickly learn new skills.

Curiosity: Geminis have a thirst for knowledge and are always eager to learn new things. They are interested in a wide range of topics and enjoy exploring different ideas.

Expressiveness: Geminis are excellent communicators. They are articulate, and witty, and often possess a way with words that captivate others.

Versatility: Geminis have a wide range of interests and talents. They are often multi-talented individuals who excel in various areas.

Social: Geminis are social creatures and enjoy interacting with others. They are skilled at networking and forming connections with people from all walks of life.

Charming: Geminis are known for their natural charm and wit. They are engaging conversationalists and know how to put people at ease.

Energetic: Geminis have boundless energy and enthusiasm. They are always on the go, seeking new experiences and adventures.

Quick Thinkers: Geminis are quick thinkers and excellent problem solvers. They can think on their feet and come up with creative solutions to problems.

Restless: Geminis can be restless at times. They may get bored easily and seek novelty and variety in their pursuits.

Intellectual: Geminis are intelligent individuals with a strong intellectual bent. They enjoy engaging in stimulating debates and discussions.

Changeable: Geminis can be changeable in their moods and opinions. They may flip-flop on certain issues as they explore different perspectives.

Playful: Geminis have a youthful and playful spirit. They enjoy humor and often use it as a means of connecting with others.

Inquisitive: Geminis are naturally curious. They enjoy asking questions and learning more about the world around them.

Risk-Takers: Geminis are open to taking risks. They are not afraid to try new things or step outside of their comfort zone.

Independent Thinkers: Geminis are independent thinkers. They have a unique perspective on the world and are not afraid to challenge conventional wisdom.

Social Butterflies: Geminis are social butterflies. They thrive in social settings and are often the life of the party. They enjoy mingling with diverse groups of people.

Versatile Learners: Geminis are natural learners. They can adapt to different teaching styles and environments and learn new things quickly.

Overall, Geminis are known for their versatility, quick thinking, and sociable nature. They bring an energetic and adaptable approach to life, making them excellent communicators and problem solvers. Their curiosity and willingness to explore various avenues ensure that life with a Gemini is always full of surprises and intellectual stimulation.

Introduce

2024 is your year to shine in the realm of communication! With your innate wit and curiosity, you have the power to forge meaningful connections and make a positive impact on the world.

In your relationships, your ability to connect on a deeper level with loved ones will be unparalleled. Your genuine interest in others and your ability to express yourself clearly will help you strengthen bonds and resolve long-standing misunderstandings. Expect to create unforgettable memories with the people you care about most.

At work, your communication skills will open doors to new opportunities and collaborations. Your adaptable nature and sharp intellect will make you a valuable asset in team dynamics. Take the initiative to share your ideas and lead discussions. You'll be surprised at how far your influence can reach.

For Gemini artists and creators, 2024 is a year to explore new horizons. Your gift for storytelling and expression will find new avenues to shine. Consider writing, public speaking, or engaging in other forms of creative communication to share your unique perspective with the world. Your ideas and messages will resonate with a wide audience, bringing you both personal satisfaction and public acclaim.

Throughout the year, be prepared to encounter exciting new connections. Your sociable nature will attract like-minded individuals who share your interests and values. These connections may lead to lifelong friendships, collaborations, or even romantic relationships. Open your heart to new possibilities and let yourself be surprised.

As you navigate the dynamic landscape of interactions in 2024, remember to remain adaptable and open-minded. Your ability to adapt to changing situations and perspectives will be a significant asset. While your communication skills will open doors, your ability to actively listen and empathize will strengthen the bonds you form.

Here are a few tips to help you make the most of your communication mastery in 2024:

- Be an active listener. Take the time to understand what others are saying before responding. Ask clarifying questions and show that you're interested in their perspective.
- Be clear and concise in your communication. Avoid using jargon or overly complicated language. Instead, focus on conveying your message in a way that is easy to understand.
- Be authentic and genuine. People can spot a fake from a mile away, so be yourself and let your true personality shine through in your communication.
- Be mindful of your body language and tone of voice. Nonverbal communication is just as important as verbal communication. Make sure your body language and tone of voice are congruent with your message.
- Be open to feedback. Don't be afraid to ask others for feedback on your

communication skills. This can help you identify areas where you can improve.

Remember, words are powerful. Use them to uplift, inspire, and connect. Be mindful of the impact your words can have on others, and choose them wisely. Your ability to communicate effectively can be a force for positive change in both your personal and professional spheres.

Embrace this year with confidence and let your words be the bridge to a brighter future.

January

January is the perfect month to kick off the year with a bang! Your creative juices will be flowing, so use them to come up with innovative ideas and collaborate with others. This is a great time to network and build relationships, so be sure to express yourself clearly and confidently.

Work: You're feeling inspired and motivated this month, so make the most of it! Take on new challenges and be open to fresh perspectives. Collaborations will be especially fruitful, so don't be afraid to reach out to others for help and support.

Finance: It's a good time to set clear financial goals for the year and make a budget. Look for ways to increase your income and save for future investments. Even if you can only spare a small amount each month, it will add up over time.

Love: Communication is key in relationships, so be sure to share your feelings openly and encourage your partner to do the same. This is a great time to deepen your connection and create lasting memories together.

Health: Take some time for yourself this month to focus on your health and well-being. Engage in physical activities that stimulate your mind and body, such as yoga, hiking, or dancing. Eating healthy foods and getting enough sleep will also help you feel your best.

Be careful of: Avoid spreading yourself too thin by taking on too many commitments. It's important to have a balance between work, personal life, and self-care.

Advice: Embrace new ideas and collaborations to start the year on a positive note. This is a great time to set goals and make plans for the future.

Additional tips:

- Try a new hobby or skill. Geminis are naturally curious, so why not challenge yourself this month by learning something new? This could be anything from painting to coding to playing a musical instrument.

- Spend time with loved ones. Make time for the people who matter most to you this month. Go out for dinner, catch a movie, or simply relax and chat at home.
- Take a break from technology. Give your eyes and mind a break by limiting your screen time this month. Read a book, go for a walk, or take a nap instead.
- Be grateful for what you have. Take some time each day to reflect on the things you're grateful for. This could be your health, your relationships, your job, or even just your warm bed.

February

February is all about collaborations and expanding your horizons! Your natural curiosity and outgoing nature will serve you well this month, so don't be afraid to network, connect with others, and share your ideas.

Work: Collaborations continue to thrive this month, so make the most of it! Reach out to peers, brainstorm new projects, and share your knowledge. This is a great time to learn new things and expand your skill set.

Finance: Explore ways to increase your income this month, such as freelancing or part-time work. Review your budget and cut unnecessary expenses. Even a small change in your spending habits can make a big difference over time.

Love: Nurture your existing relationships by spending quality time together. Go on dates, take walks in the park, or cuddle up on the couch and watch a movie. Single Geminis might find themselves attracted to someone with shared interests. Be open to new possibilities and enjoy the excitement of dating!

Healthy: Keep your mind sharp by engaging in mental exercises, such as puzzles, brain teasers, or learning a new language. Reading books, writing, and playing games are also great ways to stimulate your mind.

Be careful of: Avoid spreading yourself too thin by taking on too many projects. It's important to have a balance between work, personal life, and self-care.

Advice: Focus on fostering meaningful connections and expanding your skill set this month. This is a great time to invest in yourself and your future.

Additional tips

- Attend networking events to meet new people and learn about new opportunities.
- Volunteer your time to a cause that you're passionate about.

- Take a break from your busy schedule to relax and recharge. A spa day, a weekend getaway, or simply reading a book in bed can all help you de-stress.

March

March is your month to shine! Your communication skills will be on point, so use them to get your ideas across and collaborate with colleagues to bring your vision to life. You might also experience unexpected financial opportunities, so be prepared to make quick decisions. In your relationships, embrace open and honest conversations, and address any issues promptly and with empathy.

Work: Your communication skills are off the charts this month, Gemini! Use your charm and wit to get your ideas across and collaborate with others. This is a great time to network, attend meetings, and give presentations. Be sure to highlight your strengths and talents, and don't be afraid to take on new challenges.

Finance: Unexpected financial opportunities might arise this month, so be prepared to make quick decisions. However, it's important to do your research before making any commitments. Consider seeking advice from a financial advisor or trusted friend.

Love: In your relationships, embrace open and honest conversations. Address any issues promptly and with empathy. This is a great time to strengthen your bonds and deepen your understanding of each other. Single Geminis might find themselves attracted to someone intelligent and communicative.

Healthy: Engage in mindfulness practices this month to manage stress and stay grounded. Meditation, yoga, and deep breathing are all great ways to calm your mind and center yourself. It's also important to get enough sleep and eat healthy foods.

Be careful of: Avoid overloading your schedule this month. It's important to have a balance between work, personal life, and self-care. Don't be afraid to say no to commitments if you need to.

Advice: Trust your instincts and use your communication skills to your advantage this month. This is a great time to take risks and pursue your dreams.

Additional tips

- Start a new creative project. This could be anything from writing a blog post to painting a picture to composing a song. Let your imagination run wild!
- Take a class on something you're interested in. This is a great way to learn new things, meet new people, and expand your horizons.
- Volunteer your time to a cause you care about. This is a great way to give back to your community and make a difference in the world.
- Spend time with loved ones

April

April is a month to celebrate your hard work and dedication! Your determination will lead to tangible results, so be sure to showcase your reliability and dedication to your colleagues and supervisors. This is also a good time to focus on your long-term financial planning and set clear financial goals. In your personal life, strengthen your bonds with your loved ones through shared activities and meaningful conversations. And don't forget to take care of your physical and mental health by prioritizing regular exercise and balanced nutrition.

Work: April is a month to shine at work, Gemini! Your determination and hard work will pay off, so be sure to showcase your reliability and dedication to your colleagues and supervisors. This is also a good time to take on new challenges and responsibilities. However, be careful not to become overly stubborn, especially when working with others. It's important to be open to feedback and collaboration.

Finance: April is a good time to focus on your long-term financial planning. Set clear financial goals and allocate your resources wisely. Consider investing in your future or paying down debt. If you're looking for ways to increase your income, consider freelancing or starting a side hustle.

Love: In your personal life, April is a month to strengthen your bonds with your loved ones. Spend time together, share activities you enjoy, and have meaningful conversations. If you're single, April is a good time to put yourself out there and meet new people. Be open to new connections and possibilities.

Healthy: Don't forget to take care of your physical and mental health in April. Make sure to prioritize regular exercise and balanced nutrition. Get enough sleep and find healthy ways to manage stress. Taking care of yourself will help you feel your best and live your best life.

Be careful of: Guard against becoming overly stubborn this month, especially in collaborative efforts. It's important to be open to other people's ideas and suggestions. Remember that teamwork makes the dream work!

Advice: Celebrate your achievements this month and stay open to growth and change. This is a great time to learn new things and expand your horizons. Don't be afraid to take risks and step outside of your comfort zone.

Additional tips

- Take a break from social media. Give your mind and eyes a break by limiting your screen time this month. Go for a walk, read a book, or spend time with loved ones instead.
- Start a new book. Reading is a great way to relax and escape into another world. It's also a great way to learn new things and expand your vocabulary.
- Spend time in nature. Getting out in nature has many benefits, including reducing

stress, improving mood, and boosting creativity. Go for a hike, have a picnic in the park, or simply sit outside and enjoy the fresh air.

- Be kind to yourself. Remember to be patient and understanding with yourself. Everyone makes mistakes and has setbacks. Don't beat yourself up if things don't go perfectly.

May

Gemini, get ready for a dynamic month ahead! Your adaptability and quick thinking will be your superpowers in May, so use them to embrace change and solve challenges with creativity. In your personal life, deepen connections with loved ones through heartfelt conversations and acts of kindness.

Work: This month is all about embracing change and using your creativity to solve problems at work. Your adaptability and quick thinking will make you an asset to your team, so don't be afraid to step outside of your comfort zone and take on new challenges.

Finance: Stick to your financial plans and avoid impulsive spending this month. Look into ways to enhance your financial stability, such as investing in your retirement or paying off debt. Even a small change in your spending habits can make a big difference over time.

Love: Deepen connections with loved ones this month through heartfelt conversations and acts of kindness. Go on dates, take walks in the park, or simply relax and chat at home. Cherish the moments you have with the people you love. Single Geminis might find themselves attracted to someone intelligent and communicative.

Healthy: Engage in activities that promote mental clarity this month, such as journaling, meditation, or spending time in nature. It's also important to get enough sleep and eat healthy foods. Taking care of your mental health will help you feel your best and perform your best at work and in your relationships.

Be careful of: Be cautious of becoming too scattered in your efforts this month. It's important to focus on one task at a time and avoid taking on too much. Otherwise, you might find yourself feeling overwhelmed and stressed.

Advice: Use your versatility to your advantage and maintain clear communication this month. This will help you succeed at work, in your relationships, and all areas of your life.

Additional tips

- Set aside some time each day for self-care. This could be anything from taking a relaxing bath to reading a book to simply spending some time in silence.
- Learn a new skill. This is a great way to keep your mind active and challenge yourself. Try taking a class, watching online tutorials, or reading books on the topic you're interested in.
- Connect with nature. Go for a hike, have a picnic in the park, or simply sit outside and enjoy the fresh air. Spending time in nature has many benefits, including reducing stress, improving mood, and boosting creativity.
- Be grateful for what you have. Take some time each day to reflect on the things you're grateful for. This could be your health, your relationships, your job, or

even just your warm bed. Focusing on the positive will help you appreciate the good things in your life and attract even more abundance.

June

Gemini, it's your time to shine at work this month! Your leadership qualities will be at their peak, so take charge of projects and inspire your team with your enthusiasm and vision. You'll also have opportunities to explore new financial possibilities, so don't be afraid to think outside the box. In your personal life, focus on quality time with your partner and nurture your relationships through shared experiences.

Work: This month is all about stepping up and leading the way at work. Your natural charisma and communication skills will make you a natural leader. Don't be afraid to take on new challenges and share your ideas with your team. You'll be pleasantly surprised at how supportive and receptive they are.

Finance: June is also a good time to explore opportunities for additional income or investments. You might have some great ideas, but it's important to do your research and seek professional advice for complex financial decisions. Remember, there's no shame in asking for help, especially when it comes to your financial future.

Love: In your love life, focus on quality time with your partner this month. Plan some fun dates, go on walks together, or simply cuddle up on the couch and watch a movie. Nurturing your relationship through shared experiences will help you deepen your connection and create lasting memories. Single Geminis might find themselves attracting someone intelligent, communicative, and shares their sense of humor.

Healthy: Make sure to take care of your physical health this month by engaging in activities that you find enjoyable. This could be anything from playing sports to going for walks to taking yoga classes. Finding activities that you enjoy will make it more likely that you'll stick with them, which is essential for maintaining good health.

Be careful of: Avoid becoming overly

opinionated this month, especially in collaborative efforts. It's important to be open to other people's ideas and suggestions, even if you don't agree with them. Remember that teamwork is essential for success, so be willing to compromise and find solutions that work for everyone involved.

Advice: Balance your assertiveness with understanding and empathy this month. This will help you build strong relationships with your colleagues, clients, and loved ones. Remember, it's not all about getting your way. It's also about being a good listener and being able to see things from other people's perspectives.

Additional tips

- Take some time for yourself this month. Even if it's just for a few minutes each day, make sure to do something that you enjoy and that helps you relax and de-stress. This could be anything from reading a book to taking a bath to listening to music.

- Be mindful of your communication. Make sure to communicate clearly and concisely, and avoid using jargon or technical language that others might not understand. Be respectful of other people's opinions, even if you disagree with them.

- Give back to your community. Volunteer your time to a cause that you care about, or donate to a charity that is important to you. Helping others is a great way to feel good about yourself and make a difference in the world.

July

July is your month to shine! Your determination and hard work will pay off, so keep up the great work. This is a great time to collaborate with others and seek input from your peers for optimal results. In your personal life, focus on building financial stability and strengthening bonds with your loved ones.

Work: Your determination will lead to successful outcomes at work this month, Gemini! You're feeling motivated and driven, so use your energy to tackle new projects and challenges. Your colleagues will appreciate your dedication and willingness to go the extra mile.

Finance: Focus on building financial stability this month. Consider setting up an emergency fund for unexpected expenses. You may also want to start saving for a down payment on a house, investing for your retirement, or paying off debt. Even a small change in your spending habits can make a big difference over time.

Love: Strengthen bonds with your loved ones this month through emotional vulnerability and authentic communication. Go on dates, take walks in the park, or simply relax and chat at home. Cherish the moments you have with the people you love. Single Geminis might find themselves attracted to someone intelligent, emotionally intelligent, and shares their values.

Healthy: Prioritize sleep and stress management techniques this month. Get enough sleep each night and find healthy ways to manage stress, such as exercise, meditation, or spending time in nature. Taking care of your physical and mental health will help you feel your best and perform your best at work and in your relationships.

Be careful of: Avoid being too rigid in your opinions this month, especially in discussions. It's important to be open to other people's ideas and perspectives. Remember that teamwork is essential for success, so be willing to compromise and find solutions that work for everyone involved.

Advice: Use your determination to overcome obstacles and build positive relationships this month. This will help you succeed in all areas of your life.

Additional tips.

- Take some time for yourself each day. Even if it's just for a few minutes, make sure to do something that you enjoy and that helps you relax and de-stress. This could be anything from reading a book to taking a bath to listening to music.

- Set realistic goals for yourself. Don't try to do too much at once, or you'll set yourself up for failure. Break down your goals into smaller, more manageable steps.

- Don't be afraid to ask for help. If you're struggling with something, don't be afraid to ask for help from a friend, family member, colleague, or professional. There's no shame in asking for help when you need it.

- Celebrate your successes. When you achieve a goal, take some time to celebrate your success. This will help you stay motivated and keep moving forward.

August

August is a month of challenges and opportunities. Your adaptability and problem-solving skills will be put to the test, but you're up for the challenge! Here are some tips to help you make the most of this month.

Work: Challenges may arise at work this month, but don't be afraid to ask for help when you need it. Your colleagues and supervisors are there to support you. Also, be open to change and new ideas. This is a great time to step outside of your comfort zone and learn new things.

Finance: Stick to your financial strategies this month and avoid impulsive purchases. It's also a good time to start saving for larger goals, such as a down payment on a house or a retirement fund.

Love: Open communication is key to resolving any conflicts in your relationships this month. Be honest with your partner about your needs and feelings. Also, make time for quality time together, even if it's just a quick walk or a home-cooked meal.

Healthy: Stress can be high this month, so it's important to find healthy ways to manage it. Try relaxation techniques such as yoga, meditation, or spending time in nature.

Be careful of: Avoid getting stuck in a rut this month. Be open to change and new experiences. This is a great time to try new things and expand your horizons.

Advice: Approach challenges with resilience and adaptability this month. This will help you overcome any obstacles and come out stronger on the other side.

Additional tips.

- Take some time for yourself each day. Even if it's just for a few minutes, make sure to do something that you enjoy and that helps you relax and de-stress. This could be anything from reading a book to taking a bath to listening to music.

- Connect with nature. Spending time in nature has many benefits, including reducing stress, improving mood, and boosting creativity. Go for a walk in the park, hike in the woods, or simply sit outside and enjoy the fresh air.

- Be kind to yourself. Remember to be patient and understanding with yourself. Everyone makes mistakes and has setbacks. Don't beat yourself up if things don't go perfectly.

- Celebrate your successes. When you achieve a goal, take some time to celebrate your success. This will help you stay motivated and keep moving forward.

September

September is a month of collaboration, financial growth, and nurtured relationships! Here are some tips to help you make the most of this month.

Work: Collaboration is key to new opportunities at work this month. Reach out to colleagues and partners who share your goals and values. Together, you can achieve great things.

Finance: Explore ways to boost your income or savings this month. Make informed financial decisions and consider investing in your future.

Love: Spend quality time with your loved ones and show them how much you care. Acts of kindness, both big and small, can strengthen your connections.

Healthy: Prioritize self-care this month. Make time for activities that promote relaxation and well-being, such as yoga, meditation, or spending time in nature.

Be careful of: Guard against overextending yourself due to your desire to please others. It's okay to say no to commitments if you need to.

Advice: Nurture your relationships while pursuing financial growth this month. Both are important for your overall well-being.

Additional tips

- Set some goals for the month. What do you want to achieve in your career, finances, relationships, and health? Having goals will help you stay motivated and on track.

- Break down your goals into smaller steps. This will make them seem less daunting and more achievable.

- Take action on your goals every day. Even if it's just a small step, taking action will move you closer to your goals.

- Don't be afraid to ask for help. If you're struggling to achieve a goal, ask for help from a friend, family member, or colleague.

- Celebrate your successes! When you achieve a goal, take some time to celebrate your success. This will help you stay motivated and keep moving forward.

October

October is your month to shine! Your energy and drive will lead to success in all areas of your life. Here are some tips to help you make the most of this month.

Work: Your energy is at its peak this month, so focus on projects that align with your long-term aspirations. Seize opportunities to demonstrate your skills and talents to your superiors. You're likely to be rewarded for your hard work and dedication.

Finance: Take some time this month to reevaluate your financial strategies and consider diversifying your investments. This is a great time to consult with a financial advisor to ensure that your financial plan is aligned with your goals and risk tolerance.

Love: Deepen your connections with loved ones by showing appreciation and affection. Plan romantic dates, give thoughtful gifts, and simply spend quality time together. Expressing your love and gratitude will strengthen your bonds and create lasting memories.

Healthy: Try new wellness practices this month to enhance your vitality. This could include anything from yoga and meditation to journaling and spending time in nature. Finding activities that you enjoy and that make you feel good will help you maintain a healthy lifestyle.

Be careful of: Becoming overly possessive in relationships. It's important to give your partner space and trust them.

Advice: Avoid becoming overly possessive in your relationships. It's important to trust your partner and give them space to be themselves. Remember that a healthy relationship is built on mutual trust and respect.

Additional tips.

- Take some time for yourself each day. Even if it's just for a few minutes, make sure to do something that you enjoy and that helps you relax and de-stress. This could be anything from reading a book to taking a bath to listening to music.

- Set realistic goals for yourself. Don't try to do too much at once, or you'll set yourself up for failure. Break down your goals into smaller, more manageable steps.

November

Gemini! November is here, and it's time to embrace the energy of reflection and planning. Let's dive into your horoscope for November 2024 and explore some friendly advice and additional tips to make the most of this month.

Work: This November, take a moment to look back on your accomplishments and set your sights on the future. Your determination is your secret weapon for success. Make a list of your achievements and use them as stepping stones to chart your career path ahead. Consider what new skills you'd like to acquire or where you'd like to see yourself professionally in the coming year. Stay open to opportunities that may come your way, and don't be afraid to take calculated risks.

Finance: Focus on creating stability and a solid financial plan for the year ahead. Review your budget, savings, and investments. Are there any adjustments or changes you need to make to ensure your financial well-being? Think about your financial goals and start setting a roadmap to achieve them. This could include saving for a dream vacation, paying off debts, or investing in your future. Planning now will put you in a comfortable position for the upcoming year.

Love: November is the perfect time to address any lingering issues in your relationships. Open and honest conversations are the key to resolving conflicts and deepening your connections. Don't shy away from discussing difficult topics; it's through these discussions that you can find mutual understanding and growth. Remember, compromise is vital in maintaining harmonious relationships, so be sure to listen as well as express your thoughts and feelings.

Healthy: As the year winds down, it's crucial to prioritize self-care. Take time for yourself to recharge and rejuvenate. Consider activities that help you relax, such as meditation, yoga, or simply spending time with loved ones. Adequate rest and self-care will ensure you end the year feeling refreshed and ready to take on new challenges.

Be careful of: While determination is a fantastic quality, be mindful not to let stubbornness get in the way of compromise. Sometimes, flexibility is necessary to find common ground, especially in your relationships and at work. Stay open to different perspectives and be willing to adjust your plans when necessary.

Advice: Remember to celebrate your achievements, no matter how small they may seem. Acknowledging your successes can boost your confidence and motivation. Additionally, set clear intentions for the upcoming year. Having a vision and goals in mind will give you a sense of purpose and direction.

Additional tips

- Allow your creative side to flourish this month. Explore new hobbies, art forms, or creative outlets that ignite your passion. Whether it's painting, writing, dancing, or trying your hand at a musical instrument, nurturing your creativity can be incredibly fulfilling.

- In our digital age, it's essential to take mindful breaks from technology. Dedicate some time each day to unplug and be fully present in the moment. This can help reduce stress and enhance your overall well-being. Consider going for a nature walk, practicing mindfulness meditation, or simply enjoying a screen-free meal with loved ones.

- Foster a growth mindset in November. Embrace challenges as opportunities to learn and grow. When faced with setbacks or obstacles, instead of getting discouraged, view them as stepping stones toward personal and professional development. Your adaptability and willingness to learn will serve you well during this period of self-discovery.

December

Gemini, as December arrives, it's time to wrap up the year with a sense of purpose and anticipation for what's to come. Here's your warm and expanded horoscope for December 2024, along with some additional tips to make this month even more fulfilling.

Work: Take a moment to reflect on the journey you've traveled throughout the past year. Celebrate your achievements, both big and small. As you do, set intentions for the future that align with your passions and values. Embrace opportunities that resonate with your true self. This is a wonderful time to envision your ideal professional path and take steps toward making it a reality.

Finance: December calls for financial housekeeping. Review your financial matters and make any necessary adjustments before the year's end. This could include organizing your budget, assessing investments, and ensuring you're on track to meet your financial goals for the coming year. Consider seeking financial advice if you're uncertain about your financial strategy.

Love: Strengthen your connections with loved ones during this holiday season. Quality time and thoughtful gestures go a long way in nurturing your relationships. Plan special moments together, share stories, and express your love and appreciation. It's these heartfelt connections that make the holiday season truly magical.

Healthy: Your mental and emotional well-being should be a top priority in December. Take time for self-care, whether it's through meditation, journaling, or seeking professional support if needed. Remember that a healthy mind contributes to a healthy body, so ensure you're taking care of your mental and emotional health.

Be Careful: As the holiday season can be quite busy, be mindful not to overexert yourself. It's easy to get caught up in the hustle and bustle, but remember to schedule downtime. Relaxation is essential for maintaining your energy and well-being during this festive time.

Advice: Use December as an opportunity to recharge and plan for a balanced and fulfilling year ahead. Consider setting intentions not only for your career and finances but also for your personal growth, relationships, and well-being. A balanced approach will set the stage for a wonderful year ahead.

Additional tips

- Embrace the spirit of giving by donating to a charitable cause or volunteering your time to help those in need. Giving back can be deeply rewarding.

- Don't let the colder weather deter you from staying active. Find enjoyable indoor activities or bundle up and go for winter walks to keep your body and mind energized.

- Begin planning your adventures and travel for the upcoming year. Research destinations, make itineraries, or even book your first trip. The anticipation of travel can be just as exciting as the journey itself.

- Create a gratitude jar or list. Each day, write down something you're grateful for and place it in the jar or keep it in a journal. It's a beautiful way to acknowledge the blessings in your life.

Gemstones/Colors for Support: Agate, aquamarine, citrine, emerald, green aventurine |Colors: Blue, green, yellow.

Gemstones/Colors Not Good: Black Onyx, Red Jasper, Tiger's Eye. |Colors: Red, black, brown.

Best day of the week: Wednesday

Lucky number: 5

The zodiac for support: Aquarius

Good Luck For 2024

Made in the USA
Las Vegas, NV
07 May 2024

89667063R00036